# Mel Bay's Modern GUITAR METHOD GRADE 5 Expanded Edition

**Online Audio**  www.melbay.com/93204EEB

MW00453367

## AUDIO 1

## AUDIO 2

# Key of C Review

## C Scale – Open Position

**Phoenix – Open Pos.**

W.B.

## C Scale – 2nd Position

**Paradigm – 2nd Pos.**

W.B.

# Key of C Review

### C Scale – 5th Position

### Prank – 5th Pos.

W.B.

### C Scale – 7th Position

### Polaris – 7th Pos.

W.B.

## Mauro's Song

**Moderato**

Giuliani – Bay

## Reflection

Slowly

W.B.

## Heather

W.B.

# Chord Studies

The important thing in studying chords is to learn to hear the relationship of intervals within a given chord.

# Scale Building

Study the following section on scale building and constructing chords from scale degrees so that you will understand the musical theory behind the studies that follow.

# Major Scale Review

A major scale is a series of eight notes arranged in a pattern of whole steps and half steps.

| Scale Tones | | Distance from Preceding Note |
| --- | --- | --- |
| Root | (C) | |
| 2nd | (D) | Whole Step |
| 3rd | (E) | Whole Step |
| 4th | (F) | 1/2 Step |
| 5th | (G) | Whole Step |
| 6th | (A) | Whole Step |
| 7th | (B) | Whole Step |
| Octave | (C) | 1/2 Step |

With the above formula you can construct any major scale!

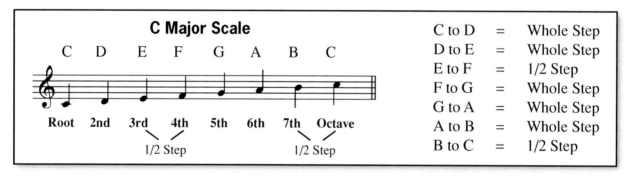

To construct a major scale we first start with the name of the scale (frequently called the Root or Tonic). With the C scale this would be the note "C". The rest of the scale would fall in line as follows.

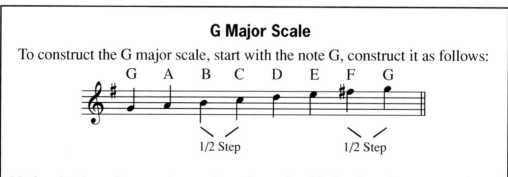

# Chord Building Chart*

| Chord type | Scale Degrees Used | Symbols |
|---|---|---|
| Major | Root, 3rd, 5th | Maj |
| Minor | Root, ♭3rd, 5th | mi, -, m |
| Diminished | Root, ♭3rd, ♭5th, ♭♭7th | dim, º |
| Augmented | Root, 3rd, ♯5th | +, aug. |
| Dominant Seventh | Root, 3rd, 5th, ♭7th | dom 7, 7 |
| Minor Seventh | Root, ♭3rd, 5th, ♭7th | -7, min7 |
| Major Seventh | Root, 3rd, 5th, Maj. 7th | M7, Maj7 |
| Major Sixth | Root, 3rd, 5th, 6th | M6, 6 |
| Minor Sixth | Root, ♭3rd, 5th, 6th | mi 6, -6 |
| Seventh ♯5th | Root, 3rd, ♯5th, ♭7th | 7+5, 7♯5 |
| Seventh ♭5th | Root, 3rd, ♭5th, ♭7th | 7-5, 7♭5 |
| Major 7th ♭3rd | Root, ♭3rd, 5th, maj. 7th | Ma 7-3, Ma 7♭3 |
| Minor 7th ♭5th | Root, ♭3rd, ♭5th, ♭7th | mi 7-5, m7♭5 |
| Seventh Suspended 4th | Root, 4th, 5th, ♭7th | 7 sus 4 |
| Ninth | Root, 3rd, 5th, ♭7th, 9th | 9 |
| Minor Ninth | Root, ♭3rd, 5th, ♭7th, 9th | mi9, -9 |
| Major Ninth | Root 3rd, 5th, maj 7th, 9th | Ma 9 |
| Ninth Augmented 5th | Root, 3rd, ♯5th, ♭7th, 9th | 9+5, 9♯5 |
| Ninth Flatted 5th | Root, 3rd, ♭5th, ♭7th, 9th | 9-5, 9♭5 |
| Seventh ♭9 | Root, 3rd, 5th, ♭7th, ♭9th | 7-9, 7♭9 |
| Augmented Ninth | Root, 3rd, 5th, ♭7th, ♯9th | 9+, 7♯9 |
| 6/9 | Root, 3rd, 5th, 6th, 9th | $\frac{6}{9}$, 6 add 9 |
| Eleventh | Root, 3rd, 5th, ♭7th, 9th, 11th | 11 |
| Augmented Eleventh | Root, 3rd, 5th, ♭7th, 9th, ♯11th | 11+, 7 aug 11 |
| Thirteenth | Root, 3rd, 5th, ♭7th, 9th, 11th, 13th | 13 |
| Thirteenth ♭9 | Root, 3rd, 5th, ♭7th, ♭9th, 11th, 13th | 13♭9 |
| Thirteenth ♭9 ♭5 | Root, 3rd, ♭5th, ♭7th, ♭9th, 11th, 13th | 13♭9♭5 |
| Half Diminished | Root, ♭3rd, ♭5th, ♭7th | ø |

**\*Note** – To arrive at scale degrees above 1 octave, (i.e. 9th, 11th, 13th) continue your scale up 2 octaves and keep numbering. The 2nd scale degree will be the 9th tone as you begin your second octave.

# Chords in the Key of C

# C Scale Harmonized

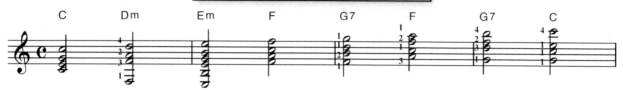

## Chord Studies in C

The following studies will train your ear to hear chord progressions and possibilities. Try playing each study by reading the notes. Use the diagrams as a reference for location and fingering.

# C Quartal Harmony

Quartal harmony is harmony in intervals of a fourth. These harmonies are common in modern jazz and contemporary music

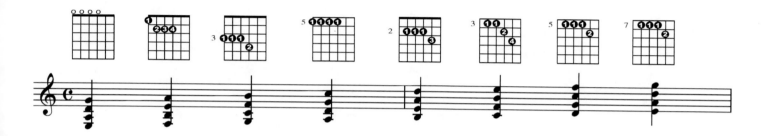

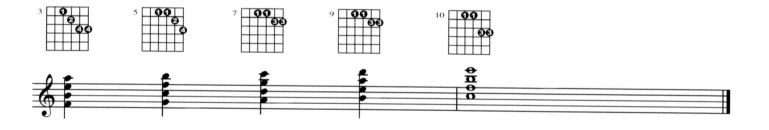

# C Quartal Harmony Studies

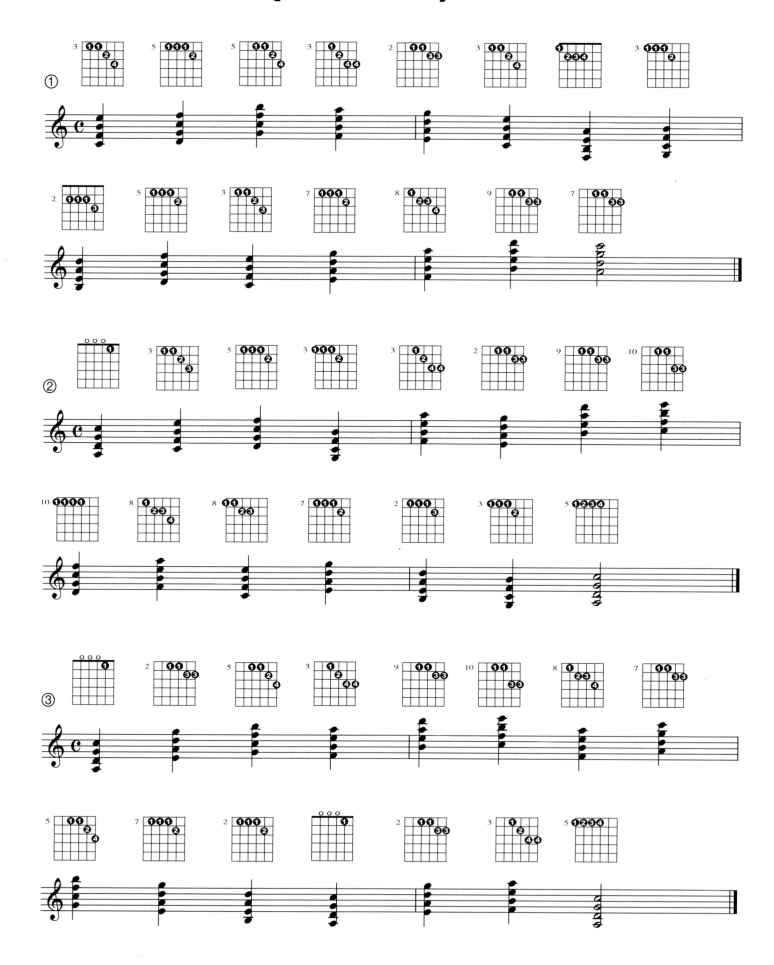

# Diminished Chords

Formula: Root - ♭3rd - ♭5th - ♭♭7th.
On the guitar each diminished chord repeats itself every third fret.
The symbol for a diminished chord is (°). For example, C°.

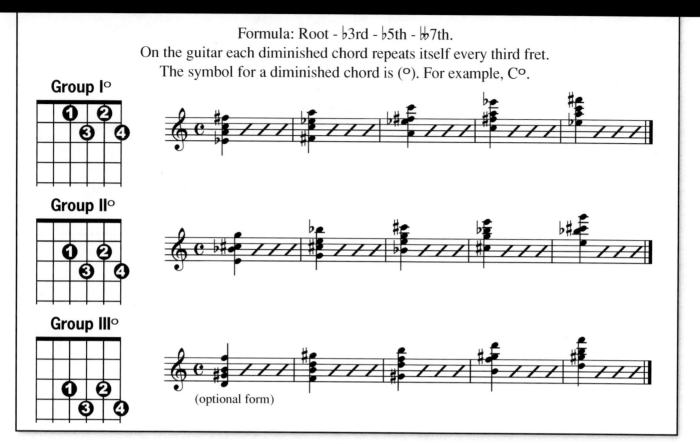

Below is the correct spelling of each diminished chord.

## The Note-Spelling of the Diminished Chord

## The Diminished Triads in the First Position

# Other Diminished Chords in the First Position

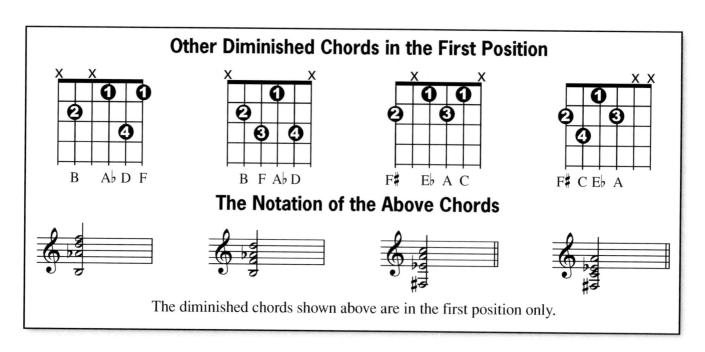

The diminished chords shown above are in the first position only.

## None but the Lonely Heart

Andante

Tschaikowsky
Arr. by Mel Bay

# Key of Am Review

### A Minor Scale / Harmonic Mode – Open Position

**Sky Dive – Open Pos.**

W.B.

### A Minor Scale / Harmonic Mode – 2nd Position

**Daybreak – 2nd Pos.**

W.B.

15

### A Minor Scale / Harmonic Mode – 5th Position

**Badinerie – 5th Pos.**

Allegro

Bach

Hold bar - - - - - - - - - - - - - - - - - - - - - - -

### A Minor Scale / Harmonic Mode – 9th Position

**Nueve – 9th Pos.**

W.B.

**Badlands**

W.B.

**Golan**

W.B.

# Twenty-Fourth Caprice

Guitar Duet

**Presto**

Nicolo Paganini
Opus 1, No. 24
Arr. by Mel Bay

18

## Twenty-Fourth Caprice (Modern Version)

Arr. by Mel Bay

# Chords in the Key of Am

# A Harmonic Minor Scale Harmonized

## Chord Studies in Am

# Am Quartal Harmony
## Using the Pure Minor Scale

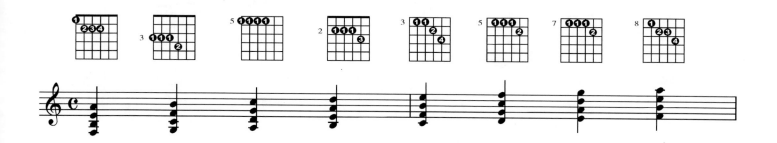

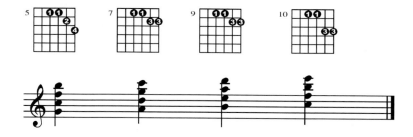

23

# Am Quartal Harmony Studies

# Key of G Review

## G Scale – Open Position

## Meramec – Open Pos.

W.B.

## G Scale – 2nd Position

## Yearling – 2nd Pos.

W.B.

# Key of G Review

### G Scale – 7th Position

### Palomino – 7th Pos.

### G Scale – 9th Position

### Sea Breeze – 9th Pos.

# Love Song (Theme from Unfinished Symphony)

**Moderato**

Schubert–Bay

# Chords in the Key of G

# G Scale Harmonized

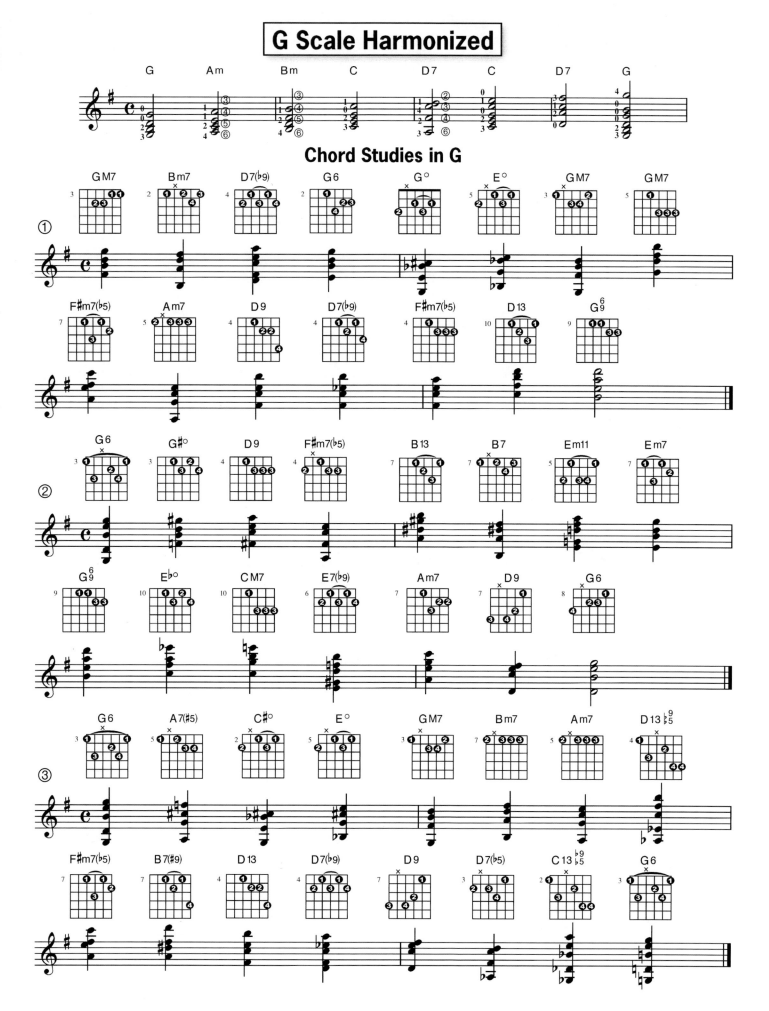

## Chord Studies in G

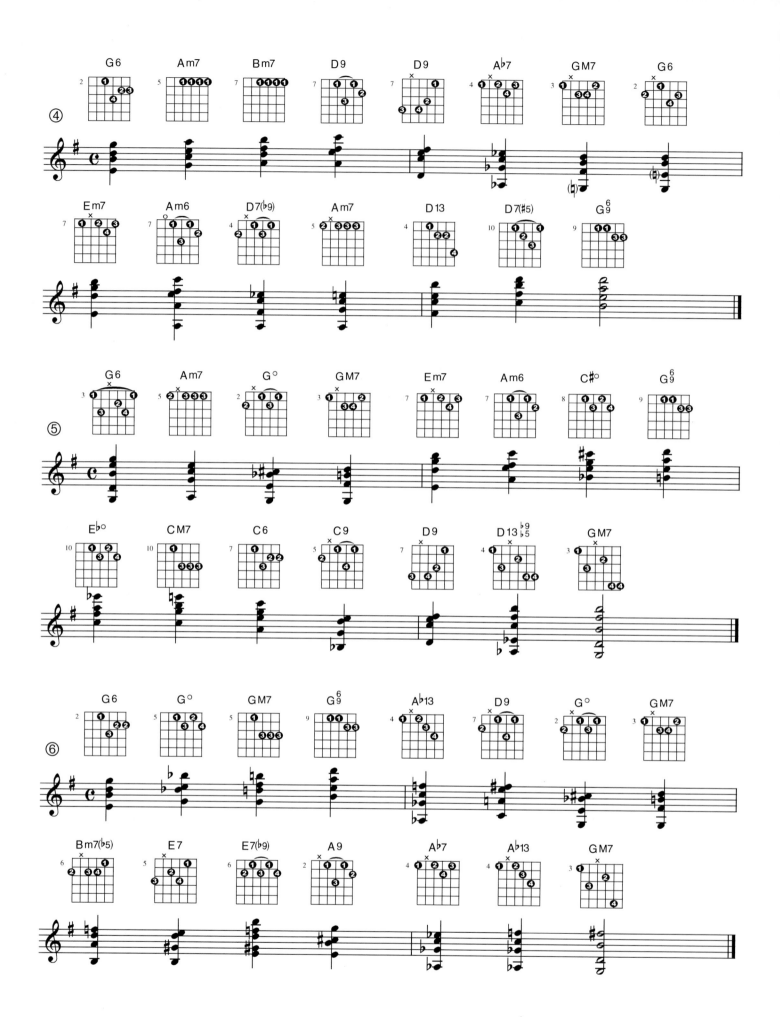

# You Tell Me Your Dream

Arr. by Mel Bay

# G Quartal Harmony

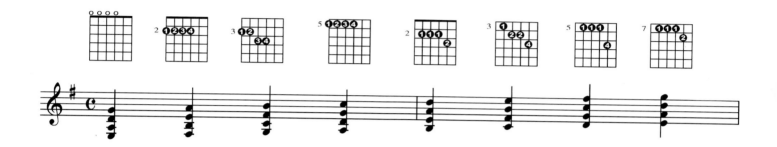

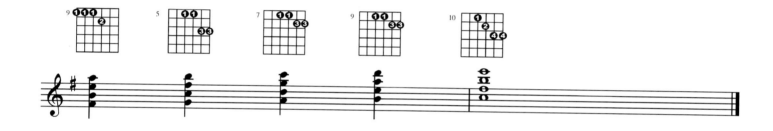

# G Quartal Harmony Studies

# Key of Em Review

### E Minor Scale / Harmonic Mode – Open Position

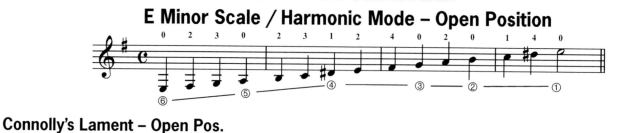

**Connolly's Lament – Open Pos.**

W.B.

### E Minor Scale / Harmonic Mode – 4th Position

**Kathway – 4th Pos.**

W.B.

# Key of Em Review

### E Minor Scale / Harmonic Mode – 7th Position

**Sketch – 7th Pos.**

W.B.

### E Minor Scale / Harmonic Mode – 9th Position

**Poem – 9th Pos.**

W.B.

# Lonesome Guitar

# Chords in the Key of Em

# E Harmonic Minor Scale Harmonized

## Chord Studies in Em

38

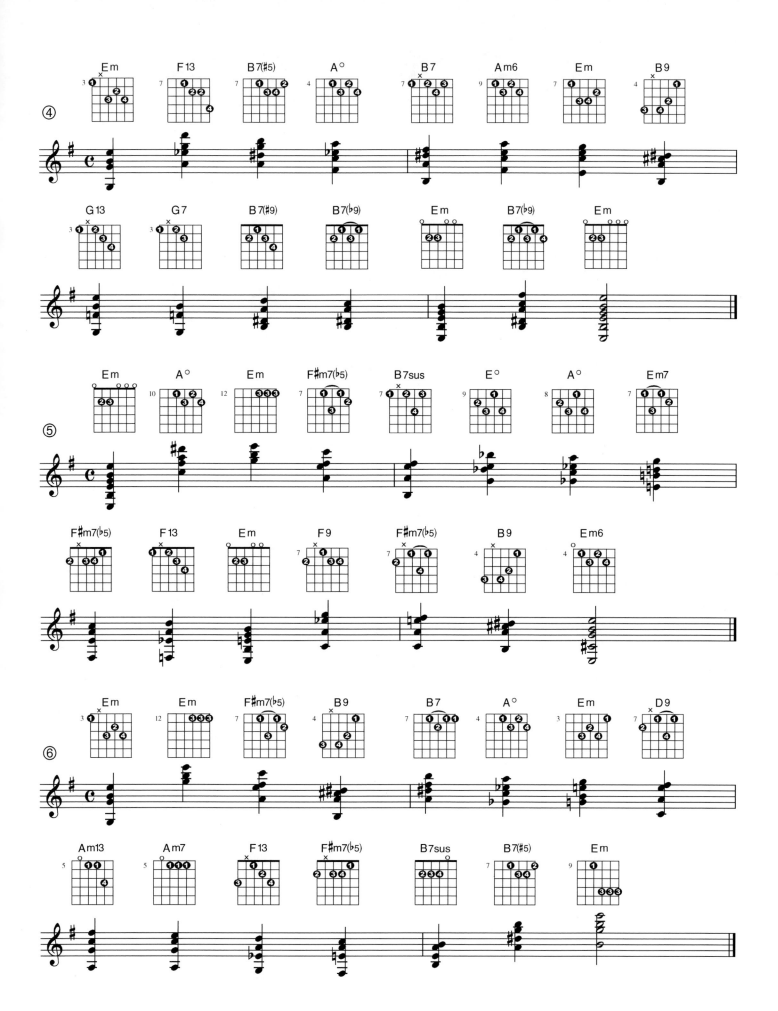

# Em Quartal Harmony
## Using the Pure Minor Scale

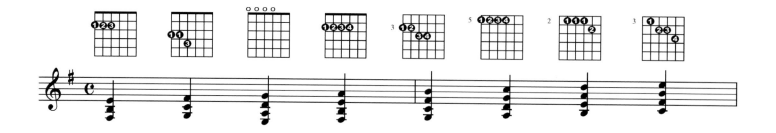

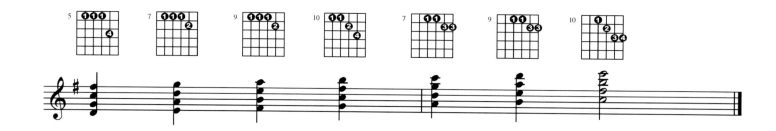

# Em Quartal Harmony Studies

# Harmonics

Harmonics are produced by placing the finger of the left hand directly over certain frets, pressing very lightly, stopping the open string vibrations. Harmonics are produced at the 12th, 7th, 5th, 4th, and 3rd frets.

Barely touch the strings at any of the above frets, quickly removing the finger as soon as the string has been struck. (Teacher should demonstrate.)

Harmonics are designated by the abbreviations "Har. 12," "Har. 7," "Har. 5," and "Har. 4" placed over or under the note to be treated in this manner. Harmonics are written an octave lower than they sound.

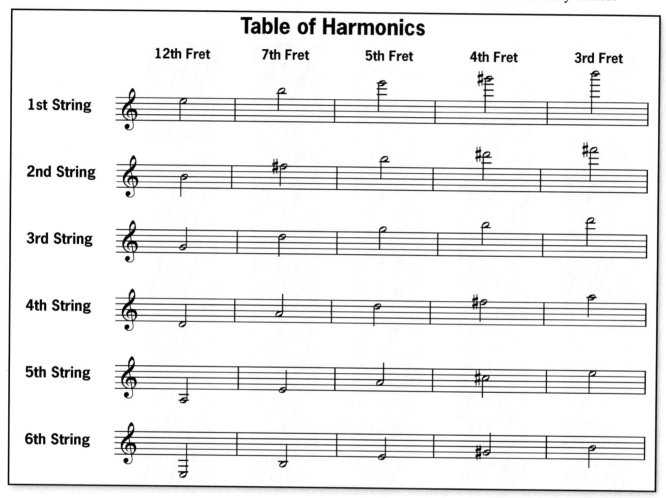

## Exercise

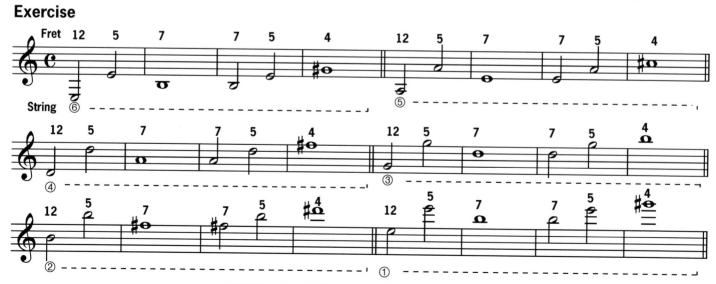

## Chime Bells (A Study in Harmonics)

Guitar Solo

(All notes in harmonics)

## Artificial Harmonics

Artificial harmonics enable the guitarist to play all notes on the guitar harmonically. They are performed in the following manner:

1. Place the finger of the left hand on the note desired.
2. Hold the pick firmly between the thumb and **middle finger, leaving the index finger free, pointing outward.**
3. Place the index finger of the right hand lightly on the string of the desired note *12 frets above de note to be played.*
4. Pick the string quickly, stopping the tone with the pointed index finger.

### Example

# Adelita

**Allegretto**

Tarrega
Adaptation by Mel Bay

# Key of F Review

## F Scale – Open Position

## Escapade – Open Pos.

W.B.

## F Scale – 5th Position

## Waterfall – 5th Pos.

W.B.

# Key of F Review

### F Scale – 7th Position

## Maple Leaf – 7th Pos.

W.B.

### F Scale – 10th Position

## Azure – 10th Pos.

W.B.

# Jeanie with the Light Brown Hair

Stephen C. Foster
Arr. by Mel Bay

## Edith

Slowly

W.B.

# Chords in the Key of F

# F Scale Harmonized

## Chord Studies in F

# F Quartal Harmony

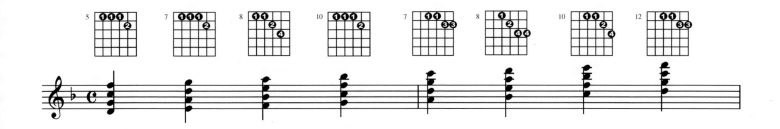

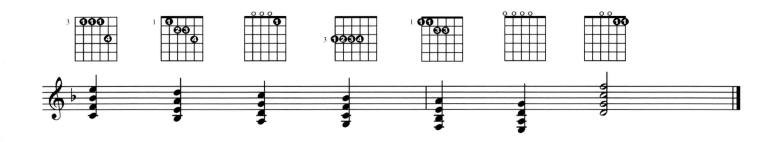

51

# F Quartal Harmony Studies

# Key of Dm Review

## D Minor Scale / Harmonic Mode – 2nd Position

**Dropped D Tuning**

In dropped D tuning we lower the 6th string to D.
Now D looks like this:

## Murphy's Lament – 2nd Position / Dropped D Tuning

W.B.

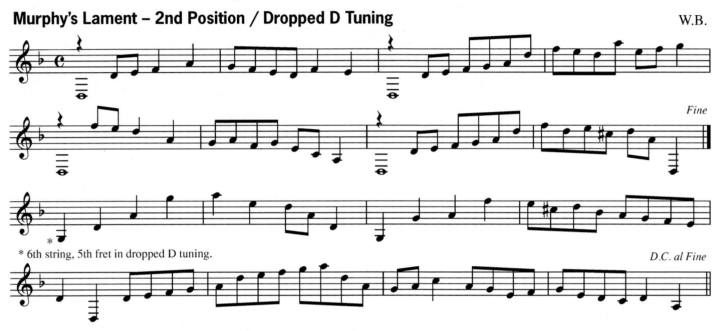

*Fine*

\* 6th string, 5th fret in dropped D tuning.

*D.C. al Fine*

## D Minor Scale / Harmonic Mode – 5th Position

## Kerry Dance – 5th Position / Standard Tuning

W.B.

*Fine*

*D.C. al Fine*

# Key of Dm Review

### D Minor Scale / Harmonic Mode – 7th Position

### Baku – 7th Pos.

W.B.

### D Minor Scale / Harmonic Mode – 10th Position

### Russian Waltz – 10th Pos.

W.B.

**Fields of Glencarnie – Dandenong D Tuning**

W.B.

*Fine*

*D.C. al Fine*

**Wondrous Love – Dropped D Tuning**

W.B.

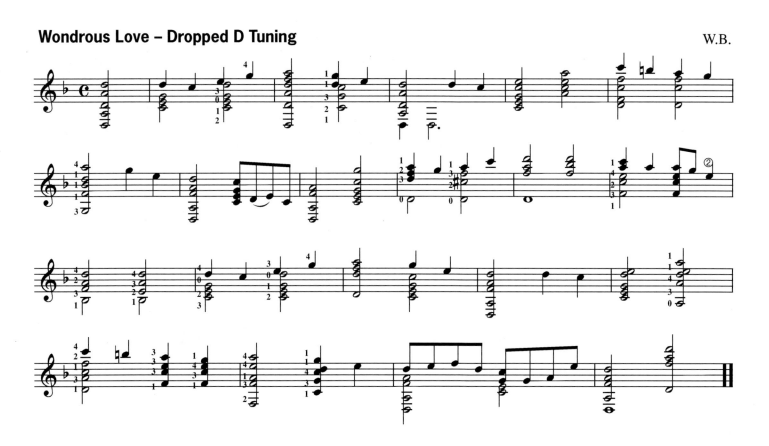

# Chords in the Key of Dm

# D Harmonic Minor Scale Harmonized

## Chord Studies in Dm

## Dm Quartal Harmony
### Using the Pure Minor Scale

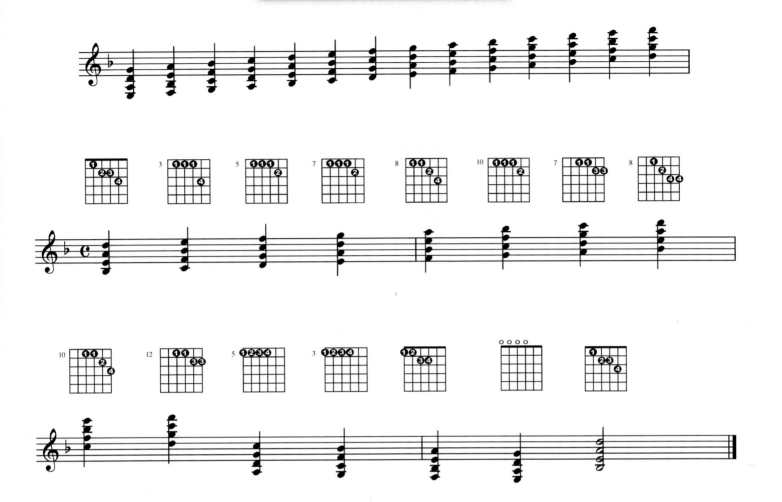

# Dm Quartal Harmony Studies

# Key of D Review

### D Scale – 2nd Position

**Erin, the Green – 2nd Pos. / Dropped D Tuning**

W.B.

### D Scale – 4th Position

**Flowers of Spring – 4th Pos. / Standard Tuning**

W.B.

# Key of D Review

### D Scale – 7th Position

**Clear Stream – 7th Pos.**

W.B.

### D Scale – 9th Position

**Wisteria – 9th Position**

W.B.

# The Augmented Chords

Only one augmented chord formation will be used at this time, but different formations will be shown later. On the guitar each augmented chord repeats itself every **fourth** fret.

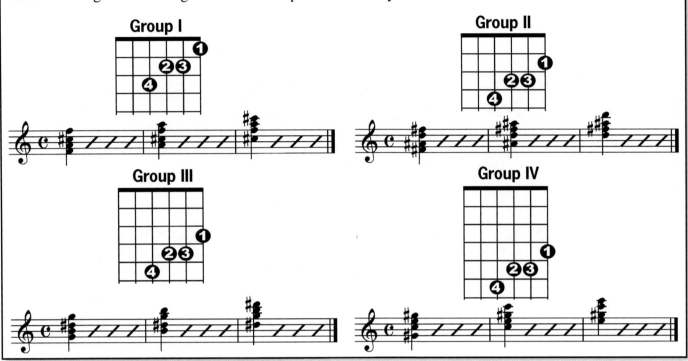

**Gavotte**

J. S. Bach
Arr. by Mel Bay

# La Paloma

Lower ⑥ to D.

**Slow Tango**

Yradier
Arr. by Mel Bay

## La Paloma (cont.)

# Mighty Lak' a Rose

Standard tuning

**Andante**

Nevin–Bay

**Special Instructions:** The above solo is an excellent study of chordal progressions on the second, third, and fourth strings. The fourth line should be studied and practiced separately until an easy-flowing melodic style is developed.

# Chords in the Key of D

# D Scale Harmonized

## Chord Studies in D

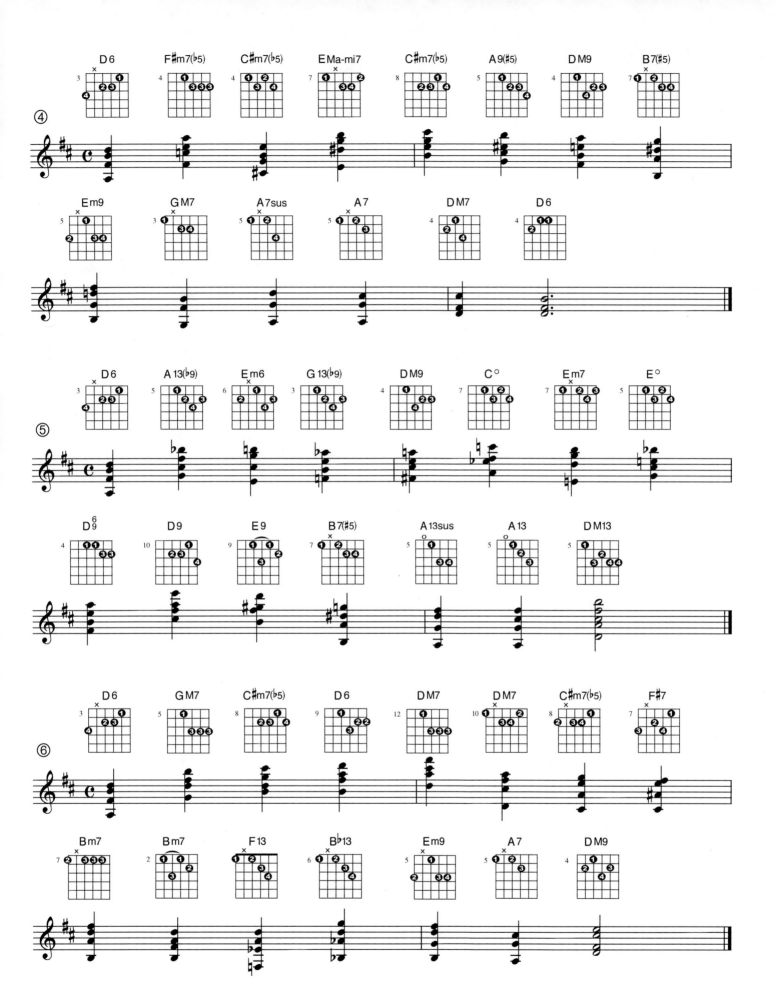

# D Quartal Harmony

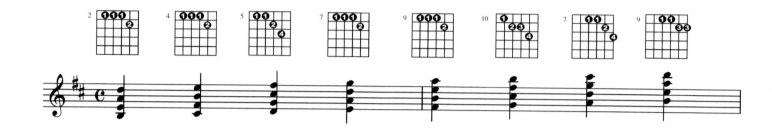

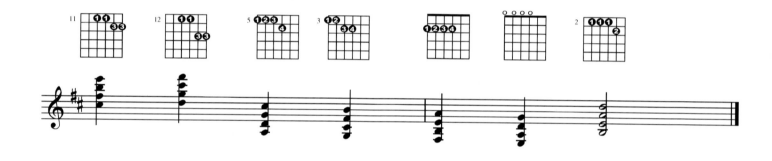

# D Quartal Harmony Studies

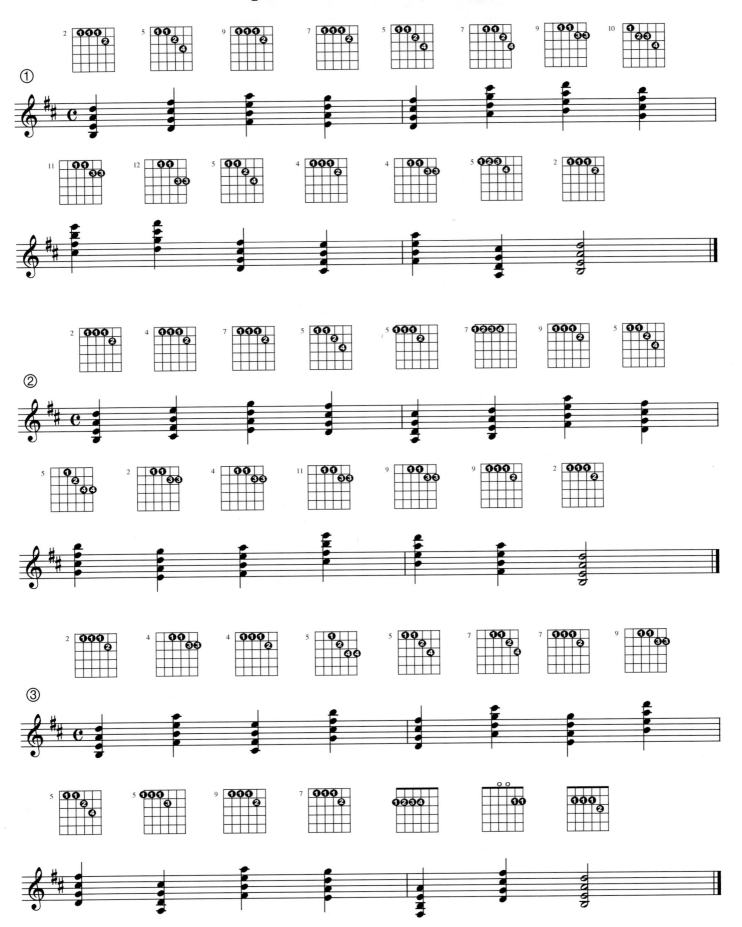

# Key of Bm Review

### B Minor Scale / Harmonic Mode – 2nd Position

**Batumi – 2nd Pos.**

W.B.

### B Minor Scale / Harmonic Mode – 4th Position

**Akespe – 4th Pos.**

W.B.

# Key of Bm Review

### B Minor Scale / Harmonic Mode – 7th Position

### Kara-Kala – 7th Pos.

W.B.

### B Minor Scale / Harmonic Mode – 11th Position

### Evening Bells – 11th Pos.

W.B.

# In the Hall of the Mountain King (from Peer Gynt Suite)

Edvard Grieg, Opus 46, No. 4
Arr. by Mel Bay

**Allegro**

## In the Hall of the Mountain King (cont.)

# Chords in the Key of Bm

# B Harmonic Minor Scale Harmonized

## Chord Studies in Bm

# Bm Quartal Harmony
## Using the Pure Minor Scale

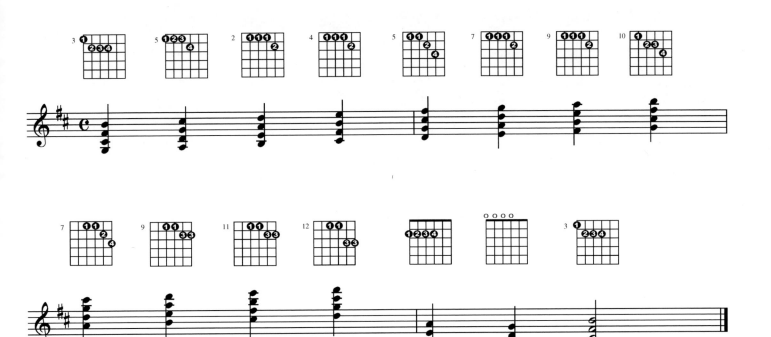

# Bm Quartal Harmony Studies

# Key of B♭ Review

### B Flat Scale – Open Position

**Song – Open Pos.**

W.B.

### B Flat Scale – 3rd Position

**Winding Path – 3rd Pos.**

W.B.

### B Flat Scale – 5th Position

## Still Creek – 5th Pos.

W.B.

### B Flat Scale – 10th Position

## Lucy – 10th Pos.

W.B.

# Reverie

**Slowly**

William Bay

# Chords in the Key of B♭

# B♭ Scale Harmonized

## Chord Studies in B♭

# B♭ Quartal Harmony

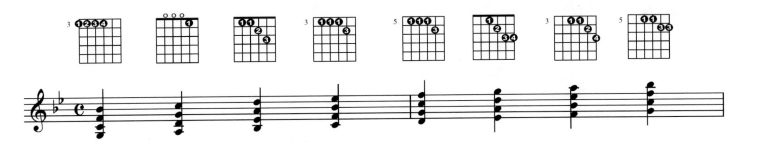

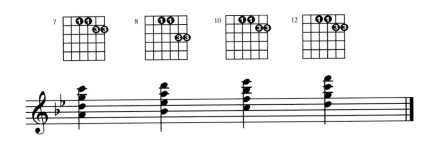

# Bb Quartal Harmony Studies

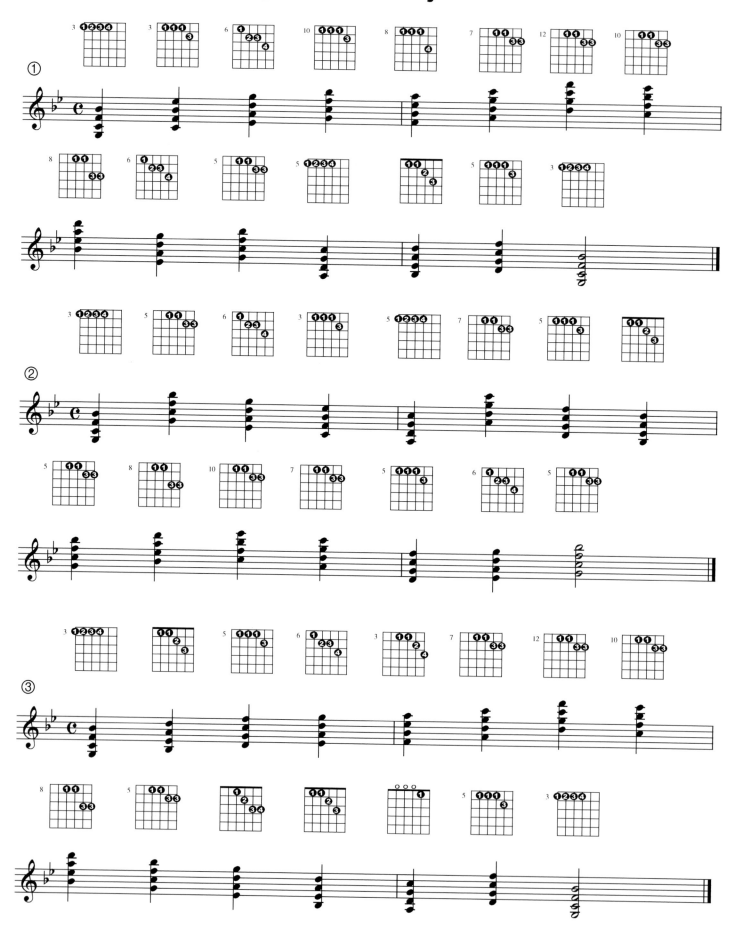

# Key of Gm Review

### G Minor Scale / Harmonic Mode – Open Position

**Invention – Open Pos.**

W.B.

### G Minor Scale / Harmonic Mode – 3rd Position

**The Spider – 3rd Pos.**

W.B.

# Key of Gm Review

## G Minor Scale / Harmonic Mode – 7th Position

### 7th Flight – 7th Pos.

W.B.

## G Minor Scale / Harmonic Mode – 10th Position

### Masquerade – 10th Pos.

W.B.

# 5/4 Time

In 5/4 Time we have 5 beats to the measure. A quarter note receives one full beat.

In 5/4 Time the measure is counted one of two ways, depending on the feel of the music.

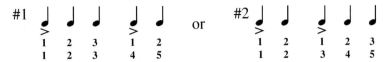

The song "Take Five" by Paul Desmond is a prime example of 5/4 Time counted the 1st way.

# Chords in the Key of Gm

# G Harmonic Minor Scale Harmonized

## Chord Studies in Gm

# Gm Quartal Harmony
## Using the Pure Minor Scale

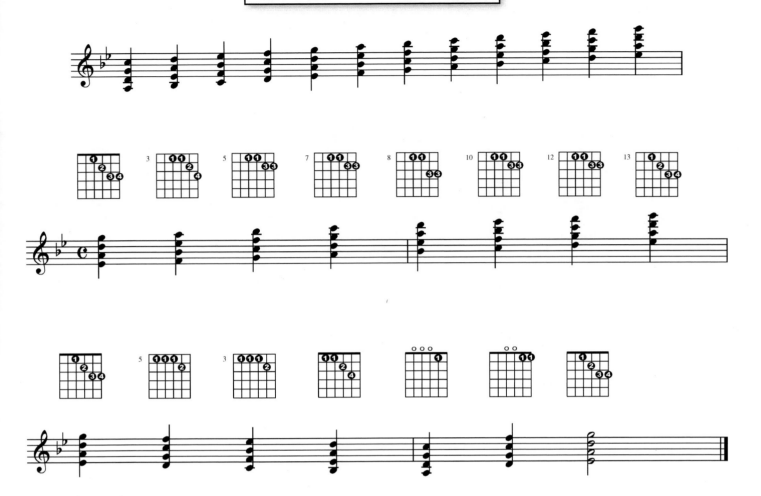

# Gm Quartal Harmony Studies

# Triad Studies

1. Memorize each example.
2. Make up your own melodies. Play every note in triad harmony.
3. Try to play these studies without looking at the guitar fingerboard.

## Key of C Triad Studies

## Key of Am Triad Studies

## Key of Am Triad Studies (cont.)

## Key of G Triad Studies

## Key of G Triad Studies (cont.)

## Key of Em Triad Studies

## Key of F Triad Studies

## Key of Dm Triad Studies

# Key of Dm Triad Studies (cont.)

# Key of D Triad Studies

## Key of D Triad Studies (cont.)

## Key of Bm Triad Studies

## Key of Bm Triad Studies (cont.)

## Key of B♭ Triad Studies

## Key of Gm Triad Studies